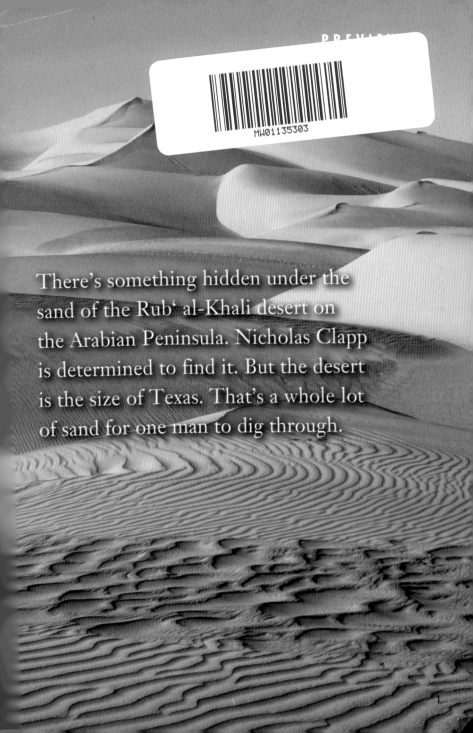

There's something hidden under the sand of the Rub' al-Khali desert on the Arabian Peninsula. Nicholas Clapp is determined to find it. But the desert is the size of Texas. That's a whole lot of sand for one man to dig through.

The Lost City

What's Clapp looking for? A legendary city called Ubar. It was said to be paradise on Earth. But almost 2,000 years ago it vanished without a trace.

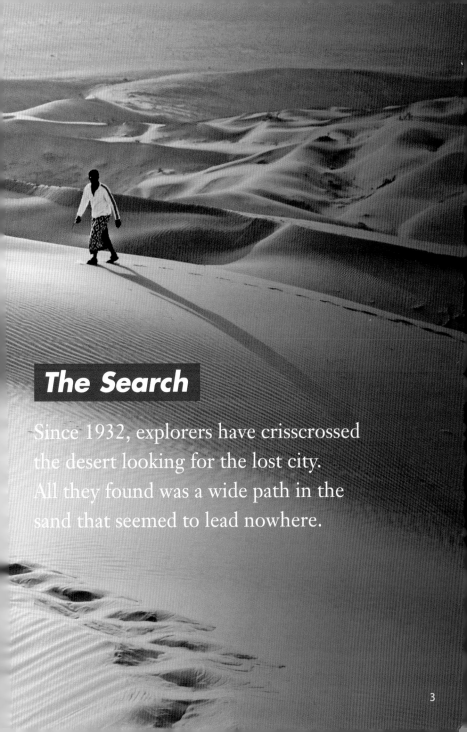

The Search

Since 1932, explorers have crisscrossed
the desert looking for the lost city.
All they found was a wide path in the
sand that seemed to lead nowhere.

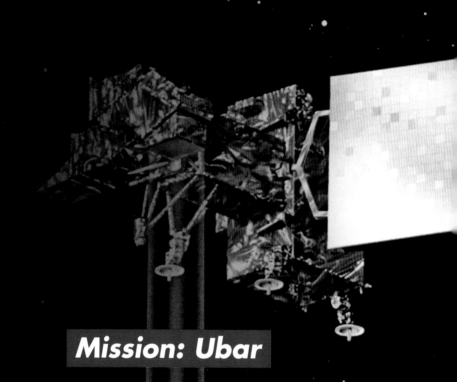

Mission: Ubar

Then, in the 1980s, Clapp came up with an unusual plan to find the lost city. And he knew just where to turn for help: rocket science!

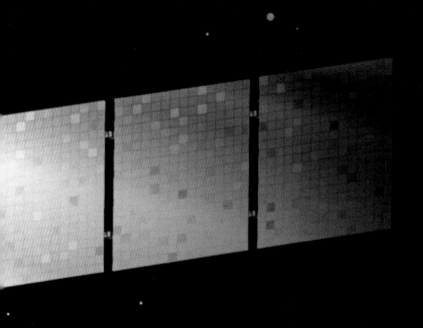

The Question

How would modern technology help Clapp locate the ancient city beneath the desert? Why are some people so obsessed with uncovering the past?

PREVIEW PHOTOS

PAGES 1, 2-3: **The Rub' al-Khali desert stretches across four nations—Saudi Arabia, Oman, Yemen, and the United Arab Emirates.**

PAGES 4-5: **Illustration of a NASA satellite photographing Earth from space in 1999**

Cover design: Maria Bergós, Book&Look **Interior design:** Red Herring Design **Photo Credits ©:** cover satellite: Andrey Armyagov/Shutterstock; cover desert: MO_SES Premium/Shutterstock; cover storm clouds: DeepDesertPhoto/Getty Images; cover buildings: Sylphe_7/iStockphoto; 1: David Steele/Shutterstock; 2-3: Slow Images/Getty Images; 4-5: USGS; 7 satellite: Andrey Armyagov/Shutterstock; 7 desert: MO_SES Premium/Shutterstock; 7 storm clouds: DeepDesertPhoto/Getty Images; 7 buildings: Sylphe_7/iStockphoto; 8: marilyn barbone/Shutterstock; 10: Carolyn Clarke/Alamy Images; 12 background: SeaWiFS Project/Goddard Space Flight Center/ORBIMAGE/NASA; 12 foreground: David Lindroth, Inc.; 13: Royal Geographical Society/Getty Images; 14: George Ollen; 17: World Perspectives/Getty Images; 18-19 background: Hoberman/UIG/age fotostock; 18 top: robertharding/Superstock, Inc.; 18 bottom: The Granger Collection; 19 top: G. Houser/Getty Images; 19 bottom: Albert Bierstadt/Butler Institute of American Art, Youngstown, OH/Gift of Joseph G. Butler III 1946/Bridgeman Images; 20: 1998 KAY CHERNUSH; 23: atosan/iStockphoto; 24: JPL/NASA; 26: K.M. Westermann/Getty Images; 27: Pat Sullivan/AP Images; 28-29 background: John Darnell/The Theban/Yale University; 29 bottom right: John Darnell/The Theban/Yale University; 30: James L. Stanfield/National Geographic Creative; 32: Media Bakery; 33: Sipa Press/Clapp/Hedges/Ollen; 34: George Steinmetz/Getty Images; 36: © Kristen Mellon; 37: K.M. Westermann/Getty Images; 38 top: Jeff Morgan 16/Alamy Images; 38 bottom: James L. Amos/Getty Images; 39: Stocksnapper/Shutterstock; 40: American Museum of Natural History; 42 left: BW Folsom/Shutterstock; 42 center: Value Stock Images/age fotostock; 42 right: FYMStudio/iStockphoto; 42 bottom: ImageDJ/Alamy Images; 43 top left: James Quine/Alamy Images; 43 top right: R. Mackay Photography, LLC/Shutterstock; 43 center left: Andreas Gradin/Shutterstock; 43 center: Tek Image/Science Source; 43 center right: mihalec/Shutterstock; 45 top: Cindy Miller Hopkins/DanitaDelimont.com; 45 center: DHuss/iStockphoto; 45 bottom: Guylain Doyle/age fotostock.

Library of Congress Cataloging-in-Publication Data
Names: Rinaldo, Denise, author.
Title: Lost city spotted from space! : is an ancient land under the sand? / by Denise Rinaldo.
Description: [New edition] | New York, NY : Scholastic Inc., [2020] | Series: Xbooks | Includes index. | Audience: Grades 4-6 (provided by Scholastic Inc.)
Identifiers: LCCN 2019029104| ISBN 9780531238127 (library binding) | ISBN 9780531243787 (paperback)
Subjects: LCSH: Clapp, Nicholas--Juvenile literature. | Ubar (Extinct city)--Juvenile literature. | Excavations (Archaeology)--Oman--Ubar (Extinct city)--Juvenile literature.
Classification: LCC DS247.O63 R562 2020 | DDC 939.4/9--dc23

Printed in Johor Bahru, Malaysia 108

SCHOLASTIC, XBOOKS, and associated logos are trademarks and/or registered trademarks of Scholastic Inc.

1 2 3 4 5 6 7 8 9 10 R 29 28 27 26 25 24 23 22 21 20

Scholastic Inc., 557 Broadway, New York, NY 10012.

LOST CITY
SPOTTED FROM SPACE!

Is an Ancient Land Under the Sand?

DENISE RINALDO

SCHOLASTIC

THE LEGENDARY ancient city of Ubar was said to be the world's largest supplier of frankincense (above), a type of incense.

TABLE OF CONTENTS

PREVIEW 1

CHAPTER 1
Paradise Lost? 10
Did a legendary city disappear? Or did it never exist?

Map 12

CHAPTER 2
One Man's Obsession 14
Nicholas Clapp finds a surprising partner for his search for Ubar.

Hit the Road 18

CHAPTER 3
Dream Team 20
Explorers on the ground get help from outer space.

CHAPTER 4
Desert Hub 24
All roads lead to Ubar.

Wandering the Desert ... 28

CHAPTER 5
Big Dig! 30
Have the explorers found the hidden city at last?

CHAPTER 6
Paradise Found! 34
Modern technology uncovers ancient history.

Gridding the Site 38

XFILES 39

Lost Civilizations 40

Digging in the Dirt 42

Hidden Cities 44

1

Paradise Lost?

Did a legendary city disappear? Or did it never exist?

The year is 1932. Bertram Thomas, a British explorer, has been trekking for days through the Rub' al-Khali. That's a vast desert on the Arabian Peninsula. "Look!" says Thomas's guide. The guide is pointing to a wide path in the sand. "There's the road to Ubar!"

Thomas knew the story well. Ubar was once a rich, beautiful trading city. A powerful king had built it. He wanted it to be a paradise on Earth. It became the world's

The Rub' al-Khali

The Rub' al-Khali desert is one of the largest sand deserts in the world. It covers about 230,000 square miles and has sand dunes high enough to be called mountains.

largest supplier of frankincense. That's a kind of incense made from the sap of a local tree. It was used in perfume, medicine, and embalming (preserving dead bodies). In the ancient world, it was as valuable as gold.

Buried Treasure

According to legend, the people of Ubar became wealthy from their trade in frankincense. They also became greedy and prideful. It was said that God was so angry with them that he made the city vanish beneath the sands.

Thomas didn't turn down the path that day. The goal of his journey was to become the first European to cross the Rub' al-Khali desert. He was afraid he wouldn't make it if he went chasing after a legend.

Still, he took careful notes about the location of the road his guide had shown him.

BERTRAM THOMAS (center) with a group of Arabian warriors

NICHOLAS CLAPP set out to prove that the legendary city of Ubar really did exist.

2

One Man's Obsession

Nicholas Clapp finds a surprising partner for his search for Ubar.

Flash forward to California in the 1980s. A man named Nicholas Clapp had become obsessed with Ubar. Clapp is a filmmaker. He's also an amateur archeologist. Archeology is the scientific study of ancient peoples and the objects they left behind.

Clapp had read everything he could about the legendary city. He'd learned about it in an old book of stories called *The Book of the One Thousand and One*

Nights. He read about the city in writings from ancient Rome. He also discovered that Ubar is mentioned in the Qur'an, the Muslim holy book. And he carefully read Bertram Thomas's story about the road to Ubar. He pored over ancient maps. And he became convinced that Ubar was real.

Clapp decided to plan an expedition to find the lost city. But the Rub' al-Khali desert is huge—the size of Texas. How could he narrow his search?

Search Party in Space

As he planned his expedition, Clapp had an unlikely partner in mind: NASA, the U.S. space agency.

Clapp called NASA. "I'd like to talk to someone about using the space shuttle to find a lost city," Clapp said.

What was he thinking?

NASA's mission is to explore space. But it also studies Earth from space. Scientists use spacecraft equipped with high-tech cameras to take photos of the planet. And some of NASA's imaging technology

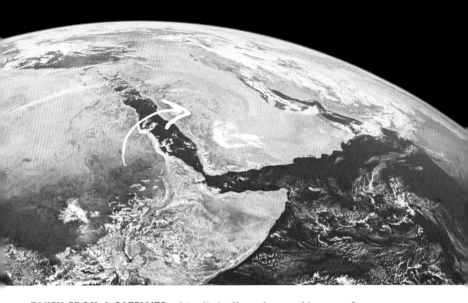

TAKEN FROM A SATELLITE, this digitally enhanced image shows a view of the Arabian Peninsula from space.

can actually see through sand.

When Clapp told NASA scientists about Ubar, they were fascinated—and they wanted to help. As one researcher said to Clapp, "What's science for, if not to find out what exists or doesn't?" So NASA researchers took photos of the Rub' al-Khali desert from outer space. Then they searched the images for evidence of Ubar.

The images didn't show signs of a lost city. But they did show a long, wide road under the desert. Maybe it was the road to Ubar, covered by drifting sands!

Hit the Road

Through the ages, these famous roads have connected people and places.

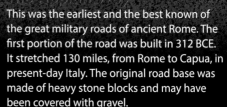

The Appian Way

This was the earliest and the best known of the great military roads of ancient Rome. The first portion of the road was built in 312 BCE. It stretched 130 miles, from Rome to Capua, in present-day Italy. The original road base was made of heavy stone blocks and may have been covered with gravel.

The Silk Road

This ancient trade route was actually a system of interlinked roads that connected China with traders throughout the Middle East.

Camel caravans traveled these routes to exchange Chinese silk, jade, and gold in return for goods such as wool and silver. The Silk Road opened up in the second century BCE and was used for more than 1,700 years.

El Camino Real Spanish for "the Royal Road." This series of footpaths was built between 1769 and 1823 in California. The roads linked Spanish villages and outposts from San Diego to Sonoma. Along the route, the Spanish built 21 missions where they tried to convert Native Americans to Christianity.

The Oregon Trail

Difficult and dangerous, this route stretched for 2,000 miles across North America. From 1843 to 1869, more than half a million pioneers walked or rode along the trail to reach a new life in Washington, Oregon, and California. One in ten of the pioneers died along the way, mostly from disease.

PROFESSOR JURIS ZARINS (standing) was one of the experts who joined Clapp on his expedition to find Ubar.

3

Dream Team

Explorers on the ground get help from outer space.

Nicholas Clapp now had enough evidence to convince experts to join an expedition to the Rub' al-Khali. His team included Juris Zarins, an archeology professor with years of experience in the Arabian desert. Clapp also recruited Ranulph Fiennes, a man described by the *Guinness Book of World Records* as the world's greatest living explorer.

Using ancient documents, plus the NASA

information, the team chose five places to search. All were in Oman—a desert nation on the Arabian Peninsula. In the summer of 1990, the team traveled to the Rub' al-Khali. The search had begun.

Where's Ubar?

Clapp's team spent two weeks in the scorching desert. They decided to skip one of the five spots they had originally chosen to search. It was near a tiny town called Shisur. They thought it was an unlikely spot for a major trading center.

So where was Ubar? The team left Oman without an answer. But they planned to return in a few months to resume the search.

A short time later, however, war came to the Middle East. The nation of Iraq invaded its neighbor Kuwait. The explorers had to postpone their return to Oman.

As the war in the Middle East raged, Clapp's team received new images from NASA. Those images totally changed their strategy.

IN 1990, CLAPP'S TEAM left the Rub' al-Khali desert without finding Ubar.

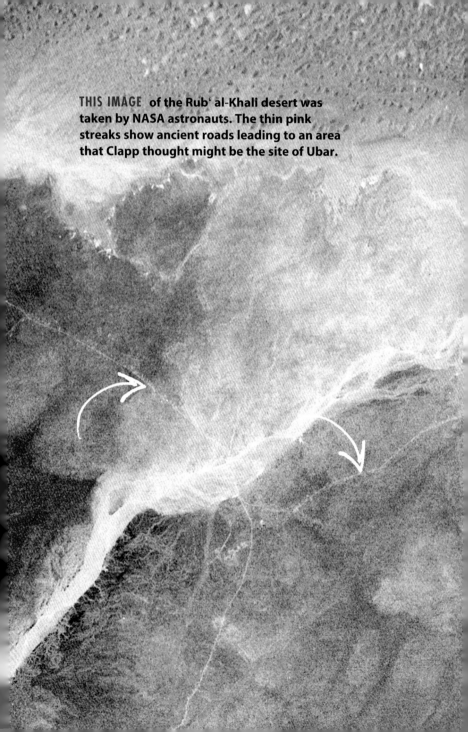

THIS IMAGE of the Rub' al-Khali desert was taken by NASA astronauts. The thin pink streaks show ancient roads leading to an area that Clapp thought might be the site of Ubar.

4

Desert Hub

All roads lead to Ubar.

The NASA images were amazing. They showed ancient roads buried beneath the Rub' al-Khali desert. The roads came from different directions and met at one center point, like spokes on a wheel meeting at the hub.

Clapp imagined long camel trains of traders traveling along the spokes and meeting up at a great trading center—Ubar!

A MAN PERCHES on a sand dune near the village of Shisur.

In 1991, the United States invaded Iraq and the war in Kuwait came to an end. Clapp's team headed for the spot where the roads in the NASA images came together. It was Shisur—the tiny desert village that the team had decided not to visit during their first trip.

Asking for Directions

When Clapp arrived in Shisur, he asked a man whether he knew where Ubar was. The man said he didn't. But he added, "Maybe not far away." Then he pointed to a spot in the distance. There are some ruins there, he told Clapp. But they were not Ubar. They were the remains of a 500-year-old fort.

Ubar, if it ever existed, had disappeared around 300 CE. It would be thousands of years old—not hundreds.

Still, the team decided to investigate the ruins. They had brought along an incredible tool. They called it the red sled. It's a radar device that can detect objects underground. (Radar is a technology used to locate things by bouncing radio waves off them.) By dragging the red sled across the ground, team members could get a rough picture of what lay beneath.

THE RED SLED, a radar device like this one, was used to detect what might be under the ruins near Shisur.

Wandering the Desert

In Egypt, two explorers discover another lost city.

Egypt's Western Desert is blistering hot. Fierce sandstorms batter the area every spring. Years can pass without any rain.

It seemed like an odd place to go looking for an ancient city.

John and Deborah Darnell were specialists in a field they called desert-road archeology. In 1992, they started exploring ancient caravan roads that once led through the Western Desert. They spent years picking through artifacts. The archeologists studied bits of broken pottery along the roads. They hoped to learn about the cultures of the people who had traveled there.

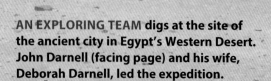

AN EXPLORING TEAM digs at the site of the ancient city in Egypt's Western Desert. John Darnell (facing page) and his wife, Deborah Darnell, led the expedition.

In 2005, the Darnells discovered something huge—the ruins of a city that was more than 3,500 years old! They found a bakery that could produce "enough bread to feed an army," according to John Darnell. And they found evidence of desert soldiers who used to fight for the Egyptian pharaohs.

The Darnells thought the city was built to control the trade routes that led to an Egyptian kingdom in the Nile Valley. "We were really shocked," said John Darnell. Building a city in the middle of the desert is another example of "the incredible organizational abilities of the Egyptians."

THE RUINS OF AN ANCIENT CITY were revealed as Clapp's team excavated the site.

5

Big Dig!

Have the explorers found the hidden city at last?

The red sled detected something 30 feet below the surface. It looked like a stone well. That was interesting, but what did it mean?

There was only one way to find out. Dig!

Some of Juris Zarins's students arrived to help. Within days, they found important artifacts— objects created by humans, often long ago. There were broken pots thousands of years old. Some had been

ARCHEOLOGISTS USE SIFTER SCREENS like this to separate dirt from bits of artifacts.

made far away, in Syria and Greece. The team knew they had found the home of an ancient people who had traded with foreigners. *Like the people of Ubar.*

Staying Calm

Next the diggers uncovered a wall, then a tower. Soon the outline of an eight-sided fortress was revealed. A 30-foot tower had stood at each corner. The fortress had enclosed a small city. Inside the walls, team members found unusual artifacts. They discovered tools that had been used to turn tree sap into frankincense. *And Ubar was famous for its frankincense.*

"The pieces were fitting," Clapp later told *People* magazine. "But we didn't want to jump up and down and shout, 'Ubar! Ubar!' We were afraid we might break the spell."

THE TEAM uncovered the walls of an eight-sided fortress.

THE LAYOUT OF THE RUINS at Shisur matched the descriptions of Ubar in ancient texts.

6

Paradise Found!

Modern technology uncovers ancient history.

Had the team found Ubar? Almost certainly. The layout of the walled city matched the legends. And the site dated from when Ubar would have existed.

The archeologists also found evidence of the trade caravans that had traveled to and from Ubar. They found buried remains of campfires at hundreds of sites around the city. The campfires marked the places where traders had spent the night before

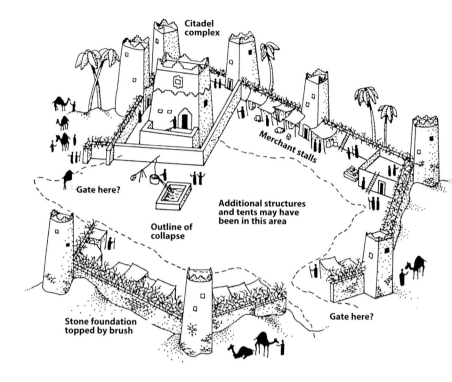

THIS ILLUSTRATION SHOWS what Ubar might have looked like. It included a fortress surrounded by a wall connecting eight or more towers.

heading back out across the desert.

Even the way the city had disappeared echoed the ancient legends. Ubar really had sunk into the earth. The dig revealed a huge limestone cavern under the walled city. Scientists think the city was destroyed when it collapsed into the cavern, which had probably once been filled with water.

Brain Power

After thousands of years, the legendary city had finally been found. NASA's technology had helped solve the ancient mystery. But according to Professor Zarins, the success of the mission was the result of something much more basic, "Brains!" By putting their heads together to make sense of evidence from a huge variety of sources, the team members had made a historic discovery. **X**

THE RUINS OF UBAR

Gridding the Site

During a dig, archeologists keep track of where every artifact is found. Here's how they do it.

A VOLUNTEER at a dig in Great Britain copies a grid on the ground onto graph paper.

AN ARCHEOLOGIST grids a site on Easter Island in the southeastern Pacific Ocean. She measures each square carefully and uses string and wooden stakes to create a grid.

1. Create a grid of equal-sized squares on the ground. It should look like a giant piece of graph paper. Give each square its own number.

2. Now copy this grid onto a piece of graph paper. Each square on the paper represents a square on the dig site.

3. When an artifact is found, label it with the number of the square in which it was found. On the graph paper, note where the artifact was found.

4. Later, you can consult the graph paper to see where each artifact was found. And archeologists in the future can consult these grids to review the history of the dig.

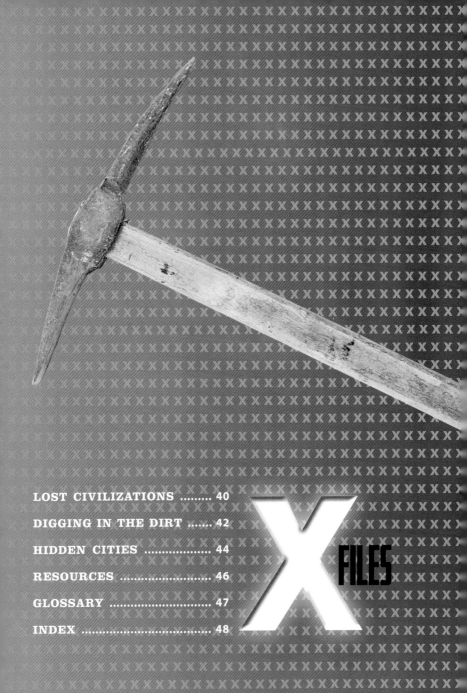

LOST CIVILIZATIONS 40

DIGGING IN THE DIRT 42

HIDDEN CITIES 44

RESOURCES 46

GLOSSARY 47

INDEX 48

X FILES

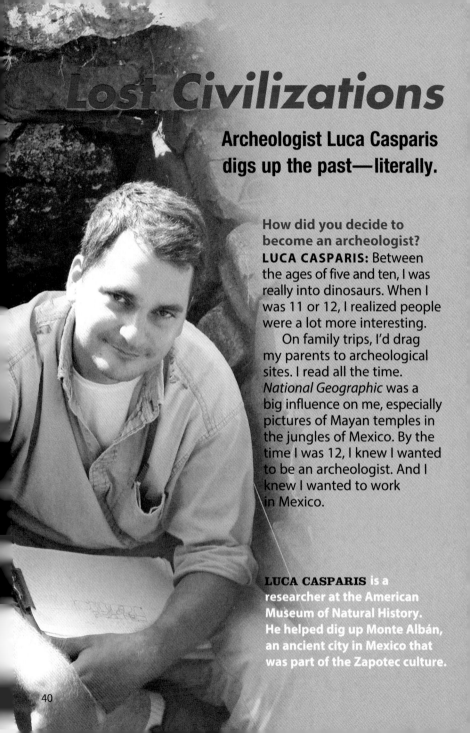

Lost Civilizations

Archeologist Luca Casparis digs up the past—literally.

How did you decide to become an archeologist?
LUCA CASPARIS: Between the ages of five and ten, I was really into dinosaurs. When I was 11 or 12, I realized people were a lot more interesting.

On family trips, I'd drag my parents to archeological sites. I read all the time. *National Geographic* was a big influence on me, especially pictures of Mayan temples in the jungles of Mexico. By the time I was 12, I knew I wanted to be an archeologist. And I knew I wanted to work in Mexico.

LUCA CASPARIS is a researcher at the American Museum of Natural History. He helped dig up Monte Albán, an ancient city in Mexico that was part of the Zapotec culture.

What's the best part of your job?
CASPARIS: The fieldwork. You try to come up with a good picture of what life was like and what people did. It's very slow and very detailed, and it's also very exciting.

What is the most amazing thing you've found?
CASPARIS: We were excavating a temple that was built of adobe [clay] bricks. In one area we found a whole set of human footprints—from people who'd built the temple 1,500 years ago! It must have rained one day while they were working and the clay got wet. It was such a direct connection to people back then.

Did you put your feet in the footprints?
CASPARIS: Of course! I'm a size 12 shoe, and they were about a size eight. People were shorter back then.

Is your work ever dangerous?
CASPARIS: No, Oaxaca [a state in Mexico] is fairly safe. The only major danger in the area is killer bees. There are snakes, and there are tarantulas, but other than that, we've never had any problems.

Do local people work on the dig with you?
CASPARIS: Yes, and it's great because they're the descendants of the people who built the city. They have a direct connection and direct knowledge. Sometimes we'll find an artifact and be puzzled by it. They'll say, "Oh, yeah. You use it for water. My grandfather had one."

What's your advice for people who are thinking about a career in archeology?
CASPARIS: Read a lot and learn a foreign language. Visit archeological sites and museums. When you get to high school, volunteer on a dig. There is archeology going on in every state. Half of what I know I learned in the field. It's not just the books.

Digging in the Dirt

Here's a look at some of an archeologist's tools of the trade.

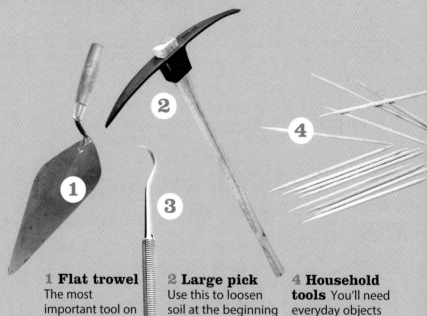

1 Flat trowel
The most important tool on many digs. Use it to carefully scrape away layer after layer of earth.

2 Large pick
Use this to loosen soil at the beginning of a dig. But don't just swing away. Work carefully so you don't destroy important artifacts.

3 Hand pick
This small tool is good for delicate jobs.

4 Household tools You'll need everyday objects like toothpicks, toothbrushes, and spoons to uncover artifacts.

5 Sifter screen
This tool separates dirt from tiny bits of broken artifacts.

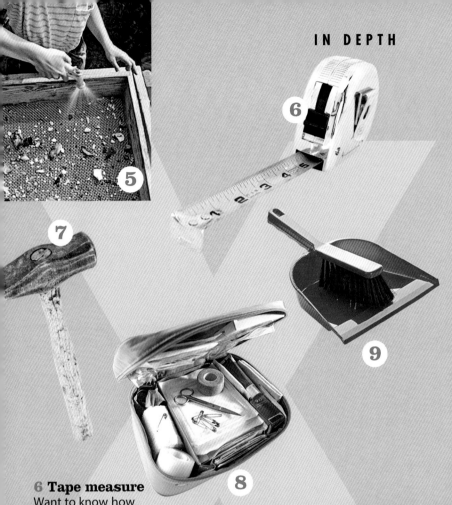

6 Tape measure
Want to know how tall that ancient wall is? You'll need a good tape measure.

7 Sledgehammer
Use this to break up large rocks at the beginning of a dig.

8 First aid kit
You'll need sunscreen, bandages, antiseptic for cuts, and medicine in case you're bitten by a poisonous spider or snake.

9 Whisk broom and dust pan
The whisk broom is for brushing away dirt from your finds. The dust pan collects the dirt so you can sift it for small artifacts.

Hidden Cities

>> Lost: Troy

According to mythology, the ancient Greeks destroyed Troy at the end of the Trojan War.

The war started when Paris, a Trojan prince, fell in love with Helen, the wife of a Greek king. The couple fled to Troy, followed by Helen's furious husband, along with 100,000 soldiers and 1,000 ships. The Greeks destroyed Troy by sneaking through the city gates inside a giant, hollow wooden horse. The Greek writer Homer told this story in a long poem called *The Iliad*. But did the city ever really exist?

>> Lost: Pompeii

Pompeii was a busy seaside city in the Roman Empire. Wealthy people from Rome spent their summers there. But in 79 CE, a volcano called Mount Vesuvius erupted. It buried Pompeii under a thick blanket of ash. Centuries passed, and most people forgot about the city.

>> Lost: Vilcabamba

From about 1200 to 1572, the Inca Empire controlled most of western South America. They had an advanced culture, rich agriculture, and a strong government. They built an elaborate system of roads and created beautiful art and architecture.

Starting in 1532, Spanish conquistador Francisco Pizarro conquered much of the empire. A leader named Manco Inca and thousands of his followers fled to the mountain city of Vilcabamba. From there, they fought the Spanish for about 30 years.

No one knew whether these ancient cities actually existed—until archeologists uncovered them.

>> Found: In modern-day Turkey

In 1871, Heinrich Schliemann found the ruins of a city in present-day Turkey. Archeologists later discovered that nine cities had been built on the same site over 2,500 years. The seventh one dates from around 1200 BCE. That's when the Trojan War would have taken place. And the ruins show that the city really *was* destroyed in a war.

>> Found: In modern-day Italy

Throughout history, farmers living near Mount Vesuvius have found artifacts that appear to have come from Pompeii. In 1748, archeologists began to dig up the city. Volcanic ash had preserved many buildings and artifacts. Today, visitors can walk on the ancient streets of Pompeii and see what life was like in the Roman Empire.

>> Found: Machu Picchu, in modern-day Peru

In 1911, American explorer Hiram Bingham set out to find Vilcabamba. Instead, he stumbled upon Machu Picchu, the ruins of a mountaintop city of temples and palaces. Bingham later discovered the ruins of Vilcabamba, but that city was not as spectacular as Machu Picchu.

RESOURCES

Here's a selection of books for more information about archeology and lost cities.

What to Read Next

NONFICTION

Barber, Nicola. *Lost Cities (Treasure Hunters)*. Chicago: Raintree Press, 2013.

Berger, Lee R. *The Skull in the Rock: How a Scientist, a Boy, and Google Earth Opened a New Window on Human Origins*. Washington, D.C.: National Geographic, 2012.

Hughes, Susan. *Case Closed?: Nine Mysteries Unlocked by Modern Science*. Toronto: Kids Can Press, 2013.

Newman, Sandra. *The Inca Empire* (A True Book: Ancient Civilizations). New York: Scholastic, 2010.

O'Shei, Tim. *Secrets of Pompeii: Buried City of Ancient Rome*. North Mankato, Minnesota: Capstone Press, 2014.

Schlitz, Laura Amy. *The Hero Schliemann: The Dreamer Who Dug for Troy*. Somerville, Maryland: Candlewick Press, 2013.

Stine, Megan. *Where is Machu Picchu?* New York: Penguin Workshop, 2018.

FICTION

Fairstein, Linda A. *Digging for Trouble* (The Devlin Quick Mysteries). New York: Dial Books for Young Readers, 2017.

Narayan, Natasha. *The Maharajah's Monkey* (A Kit Salter Adventure). London: Quercus Books, 2010.

Patterson, James. *Treasure Hunters: Quest for the City of Gold*. New York: Little, Brown and Company, 2018.

Sands, Emily. Egyptology: *Search for the Tomb of Osiris*. Somerville, Maryland: Candlewick Press, 2004.

Stokes, Jonathan. *Addison Cooke and the Treasure of the Incas*. New York: Philomel Books, 2016.

Tarshis, Lauren. *I Survived the Destruction of Pompeii, AD 79*. New York: Scholastic, 2014.

Wheeler, Patti, and Keith Hemstreet. *Travels with Gannon & Wyatt: Egypt*. Austin, Texas: Greenleaf Book Group Press, 2014.

amateur (AM-uh-chur) *noun* someone who takes part in an activity for pleasure rather than as a profession

ancient (AYN-shunt) *adjective* very old

archeology (ar-kee-OL-uh-jee) *noun* the study of past cultures by looking at ancient buildings, artifacts, and human remains

artifact (ART-uh-fakt) *noun* an object made or changed by humans

caravans (KA-ruh-vanz) *noun* groups of people or vehicles that are traveling together

civilization (siv-ih-luh-ZAY-shuhn) *noun* a highly developed and organized society

descendant (di-SEND-uhnt) *noun* the child, grandchild, etc. of an ancestor

excavation (ek-skuh-VAY-shun) *noun* the process of digging up and recovering artifacts and other clues about people of the past

expedition (ek-spuh-DISH-uhn) *noun* a long journey for a special purpose, such as exploring

hub (HUHB) *noun* the center of a place or activity

incense (IN-senss) *noun* a substance that is burned to give off a pleasant smell

legendary (LEJ-uhnd-dar-ee) *adjective* describing a story that has been passed down from earlier times and that has not been proven to be true

obsessed (uhb-SESST) *adjective* fixated on one thing

peninsula (puh-NIN-suh-luh) *noun* a piece of land that sticks out from a larger landmass and is almost completely surrounded by water

sap (SAP) *noun* the liquid that flows through a plant, carrying water and food from one part of the plant to another

scorching (SKORCH-ing) *adjective* extremely hot

strategy (STRAT-uh-jee) *noun* a plan for achieving a goal

trek (TREK) *verb* to make a slow, difficult journey

INDEX

Appian Way, 18, *18*

Arabian Peninsula, 11, *12*, *17*, 22

archeologists, *14*, 15, *20*, 21, 28–29, *29*, 35–36, 38, *38*, 40–41, *40*, 42, 45

artifacts, 28, 31–32, *32*, 32–33, 35–36, 38, 41, 42, 43, 45

Bingham, Hiram, 45

Book of the One Thousand and One Nights, The, 15–16

caravans, 18, 28, 35–36

Casparis, Luca, 40–41, *40*

Clapp, Nicholas, *14*, 15–16, 16–17, *20*, 21, 22, 25, 26–27, 33

Darnell, Deborah, 28–29

Darnell, John, 28–29, *29*

dust pans, 43, *43*

Easter Island, 38, *38*

El Camino Real, 19, *19*

excavations, *30*, 31–32, 32–33, *33*, *34*, 35–36, *37*, 38, *38*, 41, 42

expeditions, 16, *20*, 21–22, 26–27, *28–29*, 28–29, 45

Fiennes, Ranulph, 21

first aid kits, 43, *43*

frankincense, 13, 33

grids, 38, *38*

Homer, 44

household tools, 42, *42*

Iliad, The (Homer), 44

imaging technology, 16–17, *17*, 21–22, *24*, 25, 26, 37

layout, *34*, 35, *36*

Machu Picchu (city), 45, *45*

maps, *12*, 16

NASA, 16–17, *17*, 21–22, *24*, 25, 26, 37

Oregon Trail, 19, *19*

picks, 42, *42*

Pizarro, Francisco, 44

Pompeii (city), 44–45, *45*

pottery, 28, 31-32, *32*

Qur'an (Muslim holy book), 16

"red sled," 27, *27*, 31

roads, 11, 13, 16, 17, 18, *18*, 19, *19*, *24*, 25, 28–29, 44

Rubʻ al-Khali (desert), 11, 12, *12*, 13, 16, 17, *17*, 21, 22, *23*, *24*, 25

Schliemann, Heinrich, 45

Shisur (village), 22, 26, *26*, 34

sifter screens, 42, *43*

Silk Road, 18, *18*

sledgehammers, 43, *43*

tape measure, 43, *43*

Thomas, Bertram, 11, 13, *13*, 16

tools, 27, *27*, 31, 33, 42–43, *42*, *43*

trade, 13, 18, 25, 29, 32, 35–36

trowels, 42, *42*

Troy (city), 44–45, *45*

Ubar (city), 11, 13, 15–16, 17, *24*, 25, 27, 32–33, *33*, *34*, 35–36, *36*, 37, *37*

Vilcabamba (city), 44–45, *45*

Western Desert, 28–29, *28–29*

whisk brooms, 43, *43*

Zarins, Juris, *20*, 21, 31

METRIC CONVERSIONS

Feet to meters: 1 ft is about 0.3 m
Miles to kilometers: 1 mi is about 1.6 km
Pounds to kilograms: 1 lb is about 0.45 kg
Acres to Hectares: 1 acre is about 0.405 ha